The Psalms in Christian Worship:

Patristic Precedent and Anglican Practice

by
Anthony Gelston

Contents

Copyright Anthony Gelston 2008

THE COVER PICTURE

represents King David playing a harp, as a symbol of David, who was held by tradition to be the author of many of the Psalms, and as indicative of the music which may have accompanied psalm-singing; it is taken from a French Jewish manuscript from Northern France, c. 1278-1298, which is in the British Library (BL Add. MS 11639, f.117v. It is copyright the British Library Board and reprinted by permission.) The Hebrew text reads 'This is David playing a harp'.

ABBREVIATIONS

The following abbreviations are used throughout this Study without further explanation:

ACC   - Alcuin Club Collection
ASB   - Alternative Service Book 1980
BCP   - Book of Common Prayer
CW   - Common Worship
ELLC - English Language Liturgical Consultation
GROW - Group for Renewal of Worship
ICET   - International Consultation on English Texts
KJV   - King James Version (of the Bible)(1611)
NRSV - New Standard Revised Version (of the Bible)(1989)

First Impression November 2008

ISSN 0951-2667
ISBN 978-1-85311-976-7

Foreword

I should like to thank Jack Ryding for first suggesting that I might write something on the psalms in early Christian worship, and the members of the Alcuin/GROW Joint Editorial Board for commissioning the present Study. Early discussion encouraged the inclusion of a substantial section on Anglican practice, both historical and contemporary, a suggestion which I welcomed. Particular thanks are due to Colin Buchanan for much help with the editorial side of the work, and for his felicitous suggestion of the sub-title to indicate the scope of the Study.

The use of the psalms in Christian worship is a vast topic, and even within the parameters indicated by the sub-title only an outline can be attempted in a work of this scale. The academic disciplines of biblical and liturgical study have not always been in close contact with each other, and I have kept in mind a broad readership with practical experience but limited specialist knowledge. The brief section on further reading makes no attempt to be comprehensive, but simply draws attention to a few books in which different angles of the subject may be explored more fully.

I have tried wherever possible to give references to primary texts, and have resorted to footnotes referring to the secondary literature only on a few points of detail, or where the primary texts are not readily accessible. For practical convenience biblical references, including references to particular verses of the psalms, are to the NRSV. The numeration of the psalms adopted throughout is that of the Hebrew text, followed also in the NRSV. Readers who consult the secondary literature should be aware that some works follow the numeration of the Septuagint and Vulgate, and that verse numbers vary in different translations of the Psalter.

This work is the fruit of a lifetime's study and use of the psalms. It is my hope that it will stimulate interest in these ancient texts, which continue to resonate so richly with human religious experience to this day, and that it may also do something to stem the decline in the use of psalmody in current practice in many parts of the Church of England.

1. The Psalms within the Bible

The Canon of the Hebrew Bible is in three parts, summarized in Luke 24.44 as the law of Moses, the prophets, and the psalms. The law or Torah consists of the first five books of the Old Testament, Genesis–Deuteronomy. The prophets comprise two sections: the former prophets consisting of Joshua, Judges, Samuel and Kings, and the latter prophets consisting of Isaiah, Jeremiah, Ezekiel and the Twelve (Hosea–Malachi). The third section, often called the Writings, is a less homogeneous group consisting of all the remaining books of the Old Testament. The Psalms have pride of place among them, and have sometimes, as in Luke, lent their name to the whole section.

The Greek Bible, commonly known as the Septuagint (LXX) because of the tradition that it was translated from the Hebrew by seventy or seventy-two translators, contains all the books in the Hebrew Bible, but in a different arrangement, and with some additional books. In the Greek Bible after the Law the remaining books are arranged into three further groups. The first group consists of books of a historical nature, the second of books of a poetic or 'Wisdom' nature, and the third of the prophetical books (the latter prophets of the Hebrew Bible with the addition of Daniel and Lamentations). In each of these three later sections the additional books (such as Ecclesiasticus) are included in the appropriate section. The Psalms are naturally found in the second of the later sections.

The Psalms are not the only compositions of this nature in the Hebrew Bible. The only other complete book consisting wholly of comparable material is Lamentations. There are, however, a number of other psalms scattered in various parts of the Old Testament, such as the song of Hannah in 1 Samuel 2 and Jonah's thanksgiving psalm for deliverance from being swallowed up by the fish in Jonah 2. Christian manuscripts of the complete Septuagint often contain after the Psalms a separate collection of 'Odes' consisting of canticles of this kind, including New Testament canticles such as the Magnificat and Benedictus. These, however, fall outside the scope of the present Study.

We should also be aware that there are other collections of comparable hymnic material, which never became part of the canon of Scripture. Such are the Thanksgiving Hymns from Qumran, the (Jewish) Psalms of Solomon, and the (Christian) Odes of Solomon. These are mentioned here only to indicate that the canonical Psalter belongs to a wider genre.

There are two further features of the Septuagint Psalter that need to be noted. The first is that it contains an additional Psalm 151, which is not in the Hebrew Psalter. This is also to be found, with four further additional psalms 152-155, in part of the tradition of the Syriac Bible. No further notice of it will be taken in this Study. The other feature of the Septuagint Psalter is of greater importance. At several points psalms have been divided differently from the Hebrew Psalter, and this has resulted in a different enumeration of many of the psalms. The main difference is that Psalms 9-10 of the Hebrew Psalter are a single Psalm 9 in the Greek Psalter, while Psalm 147 of the Hebrew Bible is divided into two Psalms 146 and 147 in the Greek Psalter. These two variants ensure together that both Psalters run to 150, but the numbers which come between these two places of variance inevitably come one number lower in the Greek than in the Hebrew text. There is a further difference at one other point. The Hebrew Psalms 114-115 are combined into a single Psalm 113 in the Greek Psalter, while the Hebrew Psalm 116 is divided into two Psalms 114 and 115 in the Greek Psalter. These differences in division and enumeration in the Greek Psalter are followed also in the Latin Psalter of the Vulgate, which is the Psalter used in the Roman Catholic Church. Care has therefore to be exercised in comparing Psalm tables in the Roman Catholic and Orthodox churches with those in Jewish and Anglican usage. In this study the enumeration of the Hebrew Bible, which is also that of the English Bible and of Anglican service books, will be followed. For practical convenience verse references will be given according to the NRSV, unless indicated otherwise by the context.

It is an obvious fact that the Hebrew Psalter is the original text, and the Septuagint a translation of it. The earlier Latin translations, generally called the Old Latin version, were made chiefly, if not entirely, from the Septuagint. Jerome, who worked for many years on Latin translations of the Bible, gradually became convinced that what he called the *Hebraica veritas* was the authentic text of the Old Testament, and resolved to make a Latin translation directly from the Hebrew text rather than from the Septuagint. In fact he produced altogether three Latin versions of the Psalter, of which the first was a revision of the Old Latin according to the Septuagint, the second (the so-called 'Gallican' Psalter) was a much more thorough revision based on a comparison of the Septuagint with later Greek translations and with the Hebrew text, while the third (the 'Hebrew' Psalter) was a translation made directly from the Hebrew text.

One of the considerations that persuaded Jerome of the need for a translation from the Hebrew text was the fact that in dialogue with Jews there was no hope of them taking seriously arguments based on a text which was at variance from the Hebrew original. His conviction of the priority of the *Hebraica veritas* led him into serious controversy, and Augustine famously wrote to him asserting the inspiration and authority of the Septuagint in the Christian Church, and urging him not to abandon it in favour of the Hebrew text. Augustine's view was widely held, and Jerome's *Psalterium iuxta Hebraeos* did not displace his *Psalterium iuxta LXX* (the 'Gallican' Psalter) in the Vulgate, which became the official Bible of the Latin Church.

Modern study of the psalms of the Hebrew Bible has concentrated on three particular aspects. The most successful has been the analysis of the psalms into different categories, marked to some extent by characteristic features. This is one application of what biblical scholars usually call 'Form Criticism'. To give a simple example, one category of psalm is the hymn, consisting of two basic elements: a call to worship God, followed by a reason or reasons for doing so. The shortest psalm (117) is an excellent example of this, and the very familiar Psalm 100 reflects a duplication of the same two elements.

A much more speculative instance of form criticism begins with the observation that there is a turning-point in several of the psalms at which urgent supplication for God's intervention gives way to assurance, e.g. Psalms 6 (v8), 20 (v6) and 28 (v6). Some scholars have suggested that an 'oracle of salvation' may have been delivered by a priest or cultic prophet at this point, and that it was this that gave rise to the sudden expression of confidence. There is, however, no clear evidence of this practice, and it must remain at present a hypothetical explanation.

There are occasional indications that a psalm may have been composed for use in a variety of circumstances. For instance, it is questionable whether any single worshipper suffered all the different kinds of affliction mentioned in Psalm 22 at the same time, while Psalm 107 seems deliberately to provide for different groups of people to give thanks for deliverance from a number of different situations of affliction or danger (this is brought out by the repeated 'Some' at the beginning of verses 4, 10, 17 and 23 in the NRSV).

Attempts to detect the historical circumstances in which each psalm originated have been much less successful. Very occasionally a psalm contains a clear indication of its origin, such as the reference to the Babylonian exile in Psalm 137. More generally psalms which mention the king must date from before the exile, since the monarchy was never restored (except briefly in the Hasmonean period, which is too late for most of these psalms). Some form critics have attempted to reconstruct the pre-exilic cultic pattern in which particular psalms may have been used, but there is very little firm evidence on which to base such reconstructions. Inferences from the content of the psalms are almost all we have to go on, and there is considerable scope for differences of opinion.

Another approach which has led to little in the way of results is the examination of the order of the psalms in an attempt to discern a clear pattern behind their arrangement. It is almost certain that the canonical Psalter represents the culmination of a long process of compilation of much shorter collections. The presence of a few duplicates (14 + 53, the end of 40 + 70, parts of 57 and 60 + 108) alone requires some such explanation. It is often possible to detect connections between a few adjacent psalms, for instance the alternating morning - evening - morning sequence in 3 - 5, or the balance of prayers for the king (before and after a battle?) in 20 - 21, or the group of psalms (95-99) celebrating the sovereignty of God. Other psalms, however, such as 139, seem to stand alone both in their individual content and in their place within the order of the psalms. Yet others, which have material in common, such as 15 and 24, which both deal with the character required in worshippers at the Temple, are not placed adjacently in the sequence. One practical corollary of this is that there is no compelling reason to use the psalms liturgically in their canonical order, as there is in the case of biblical texts of a narrative nature.

The psalms are by no means the only poetic texts in the Old Testament, and much study has been devoted to the formal aspects of Hebrew poetry. The two most obvious features, which are readily apparent in translation, are parallelism and the use of refrains. There are various kinds of parallelism, but the most common are those where a second clause either repeats the thought of the first in a different form (e.g Psalm 5.1) or offers a contrast to it (e.g. Psalm 1.6). Psalm 136 has an identical refrain in the second half of every verse, while Psalms 80 and 107 offer good examples of refrains with some variation. A feature which is not apparent in translation is that of the acrostic, of which the most striking example is Psalm 119, in which the first eight verses all begin with the first letter of the Hebrew alphabet, the next eight with the second, and so on. More usually each letter introduces a single verse or part of a verse (as in Psalms 111 and 112).

It may finally be noted that more passages from the Psalms are quoted in the New Testament than from any other book of the Old Testament, although Isaiah comes a close second. This indicates the place the psalms had in the life, thought and worship of the first Christians.

2. Translations of the Psalms

The Psalms were composed in biblical Hebrew, and are still used in the original language in modern synagogues. In Christian worship, however, they are naturally used in translation, and we need to be aware of some of the implications of using a translated text.

Writing in the late second century B.C.E., Jesus ben Sirach's grandson translated his grandfather's work, known as Ecclesiasticus in the Apocrypha of Christian Bibles, into Greek for the benefit of Greek-speaking Jews of the Diaspora with little knowledge of Hebrew. The same situation had already prompted the process of rendering the canonical Old Testament scriptures into Greek, in the version that we know as the Septuagint. Ben Sirach's grandson, however, wrote a translator's prologue to his translation of his grandfather's work, in which he spelt out some of the problems inherent in the process of translation:
'what was originally expressed in Hebrew does not have exactly the same sense when translated into another language. Not only this book, but even the Law itself, the Prophecies, and the rest of the books differ not a little when read in the original.'

At a basic level it is a simple fact that languages have individual features that cannot be completely reproduced in translation. While the alphabets of Hebrew and Greek are closely related, there are a few letters in each alphabet which have no direct equivalent in the other, and this raises problems when proper names are transliterated. There are much wider differences in the grammatical structure of the languages, and Greek has a much more complex syntactical structure than Hebrew. To give a very simple example, Greek denotes the direct object of a verb by putting it in the accusative case, while Hebrew, which has no case endings, often marks the object with a preposition, which cannot be directly reproduced in Greek, or in English for that matter. Technically this preposition is simply omitted in translation; in fact it is represented in Greek by the use of the accusative case.

Differences of this nature rarely amount to any change in the substance of what is being translated. Not infrequently, however, an element of interpretation is required, which goes beyond the scope of the process of translation itself. This may be illustrated by the idiom of 'lifting up the face'. This is used most commonly in the sense of showing favour, and the underlying image is that of a suppliant appearing in an attitude of submission before a superior, and the superior 'lifting up' the suppliant's face so as to enable the latter to look him in the eye, thereby signifying acceptance and goodwill. The opposite idiom is to 'turn aside' the face of the suppliant, in effect rejecting the plea for acceptance. Examples of these idioms in narrative contexts may be found in 1 Samuel 25.35 in a positive and 1 Kings 2.16 in a negative sense, although they are not generally recognizable in English translations (but see 'have accepted thy person' in the KJV at 1 Samuel 25.35). The situation is complicated by the fact that sometimes it is not the suppliant's face but that of the superior that is lifted up in a smile of acceptance and favour. This form of the idiom is found particularly clearly in the Aaronic blessing in Numbers 6.25-6, where it is clear even in translation, and this is echoed in the Psalms (e.g. 4.6, 67.1, and the refrain in 80.3, 7, 19). A further complication in the use of this idiom is where it is used in a pejorative sense to denote partiality or favouritism, of which an example may be found in Psalm 82.2.

This example reminds us that in the Psalms we are dealing with an ancient text from a time and culture distant from our own. Two further instances may serve to illustrate this fact. In northern Europe we experience a climate with a good deal of rain, and we tend to look forward to the prospect of warm, dry and particularly sunny weather. In the arid Near East the opposite is the case. Too often the inhabitants are conscious of searing heat and dry winds, and long for the cool breeze of the evening or the 'early and latter rains' of the winter season, which are so vital for the fertility of the soil. This explains the use of the imagery of thirst to express the desire for God, e.g. in Psalms 42.1-2 and 63.1. A more specific example is the reference to the 'wineskin in the smoke', that is hung up among the rafters where the smoke rose from the fire, as an image for a person who has become shrivelled up from disappointed hope (Psalm 119.83). We are familiar from the Gospels (e.g. Mark 2.22) with the use of animal skins as vessels for liquid, but the older translations of Psalm 119.83 assimilated to our culture by using the word 'bottle' in place of 'skin', and the resultant 'bottle in the smoke' must have puzzled many worshippers.

A much more significant example may be seen in the term 'Sabaoth'. This functions as a divine name or title, most commonly in the formula 'YHWH

Sabaoth', although sometimes in the fuller formula 'YHWH God of Sabaoth'. The Hebrew word 'sabaoth' is also a plural word denoting 'armies', whether human armies such as the troops of Israel (1 Sam. 17.45), or the 'host of heaven', which in turn may denote either the heavenly bodies, especially the stars (Deut. 4.19) or the supernatural beings who constitute God's heavenly council (1 Kings 22.19). In the light of this range of meaning it is hardly surprising that translations of the Old Testament offer a variety of renderings of 'Sabaoth' as a divine name. In Isaiah 6.3, which is the origin of the Sanctus, and is also quoted in the Te Deum, 'YHWH Sabaoth' is traditionally rendered 'Lord (God) of hosts'. This rendering is also to be found in the refrain in Psalm 46.7 and 12 in both the BCP and CW Psalters. But in the BCP version of the Te Deum 'Sabaoth' is simply transliterated, as it is also in two passages in the Greek New Testament (Romans 9.29 and James 5.4), and in numerous passages of the Septuagint. In the ICET/ELLC texts of the Sanctus and Te Deum adopted in CW it is paraphrased '(God of) power and might'. In some passages in the Septuagint it is rendered *pantokrator* (= 'almighty'), which, like the Latin equivalent 'omnipotens', is to be understood rather in the sense of 'ruler over all' than in that of 'capable of doing anything'. The Greek New Testament uses this word in the allusion to Isaiah 6.3 at Revelation 4.8, where it appears in the English versions as 'almighty' or 'sovereign'. This example has been discussed at some length because it illustrates the way in which interpretation and usage can play a part in determining the translation of a particular term, which need not be identical in all the passages where it occurs.

The need that is felt to offer interpretation can sometimes go further, as in the celebrated instance of Psalm 96.10. The Hebrew text is translated straightforwardly in the CW Psalter: 'Tell it out among the nations that the Lord is king', where the divine name YHWH is rendered in accordance with Hebrew tradition as 'the Lord'. Christians using Psalm 96, however, not unnaturally came to interpret 'the Lord' more specifically as Christ, in accordance with his designation as 'Lord' in Acts 2.36. Devout meditation suggested the further thought, in line with the Fourth Gospel (see especially John 19.19), that the focus of Christ's kingly reign is the Cross. So it came about that in some very early Greek and Latin texts of the Psalm the words 'from the tree' were added as a gloss on 'is king' or 'reigns'. This tradition is reflected in the great Passiontide hymn *Vexilla Regis* of Venantius Fortunatus, which includes the verse:

Impleta sunt quae concinit
David fideli carmine
Dicendo nationibus
Regnavit a ligno Deus.

This is rendered in CW *Daily Prayer* (p. 257):

Fulfilled is now what David told
in true prophetic song of old,
how God the nations' King should be;
for God is reigning from the tree.

No modern scholar would claim for a moment that the words 'from the tree' formed part of the original text of Psalm 96. Yet in the mid-second century this phrase became a bone of contention between Jew and Christian, as may be seen in the writings of Justin Martyr: *1 Apology* 41 and *Dialogue with Trypho the Jew* 73. The second of these passages is particularly instructive, since it occurs in the context of Justin's argument that the Jews had falsified the text of the Old Testament by deliberately omitting passages which Justin claimed proved the truth of the Christian affirmations about Christ. At the end of chapter 71 Trypho not unreasonably asks Justin to give some examples of passages which he claims have been deliberately omitted from the Hebrew text, and the citation from Psalm 96.10 is the fourth of the instances adduced by Justin in reply.

Apart from its intrinsic interest in the history of Christian interpretation of the Psalms, this example draws attention to the fact that there are textual variants of varying value in the manuscript tradition of both the Hebrew text of the Old Testament and the ancient translations of it into Greek, Latin, Aramaic and Syriac, so that differences between one English translation and another are sometimes due to textual variants rather than to alternative interpretations. In particular, as we shall see, the BCP Psalter derives essentially from a translation of the Septuagint rather than of the Hebrew text, and inevitably perpetuates many of the textual errors of that version. A very clear example of a difference of a textual kind is to be seen in the BCP text of Psalm 14, where verses 5-7 have no counterpart in the Hebrew text, but derive from a catena of texts in Romans 3.13-18, following an abridged citation of Psalm 14.1b-3 in verses 10-12. This catena came into the Septuagint text of Psalm 14 at an early date, and from there into the Vulgate, from which the BCP Psalter was translated.

The disappearance of these verses from more modern translations of Psalm 14, even as early as the KJV, simply reflects the textual judgement that they are not part of the original text of the Psalm.

Another issue affecting the accuracy of translation arises in connection with the culture of the environment for which the translation is being made. This may be illustrated from recent history in the case of the problems raised by inclusive language during the period since the publication of the ASB in 1980. The terms 'son of man / sons of men', 'man', and 'mankind' have generally been replaced in the CW Psalter by such expressions as 'all mortal flesh' (36.7), 'the peoples / the whole human race' (62.9), and 'mortals / mere human beings' (144.3). At 44.1 'our fathers' has become 'our forebears'; at 104.15 'for the service of mankind' has become 'to meet our needs'; and at 146.2 'son of man' is rendered in the abstract: 'any human power'. Similarly, the generic use of 'the man that / who ... ', as, e.g., in Ps. 1.1, is replaced by the plural pronoun 'they who ...'. Such translations, regarded as a necessary concession to current political correctness, are of course technically inaccurate, but it may well be felt that they express the meaning of the Hebrew text faithfully in a modern idiom.

At the same time it will not have escaped the discerning that the CW Psalter contains two versions of Psalm 8. In the first version verse 5 follows the Hebrew text literally, providing 'man ... the son of man', while the second version paraphrases this as 'mortals ... mere human beings'. The reason for the apparent concession to tradition in the first version is the important citation of this part of the Psalm in Hebrews 2.6-10, where the phrase 'son of man' receives a Christological exegesis, in keeping with the use of this expression by Jesus with reference to himself in the Gospels. This introduces a further dimension into the complexities of translation of the Psalms for use in Christian worship.

Psalm 8 affords an illustration of another difficulty for translators. The commonest word for 'God' in biblical Hebrew is *Elohim*, which in form is a plural noun. While in the great majority of passages it denotes the one God of normative Israelite belief, there are passages where it refers to the many gods of pagan culture, or simply to any kind of supernatural being, such as the ghost of Samuel brought up by the medium at Endor (1 Sam. 28.13; the NRSV translates 'a divine being', but the context identifies it clearly as the deceased Samuel). In three passages of Job (1.6, 2.1, and 38.7) mention is made of heavenly beings who are designated 'sons of

God', but in the Septuagint they are not unreasonably rendered as 'angels'. *Elohim* is similarly rendered 'angels' in the Septuagint in three passages of the Psalms (8.5, 97.7, and 138.1 - NRSV references), although only in the first of these does the CW Psalter (in both its versions of Ps.8) also render the word 'angels', doubtless reflecting again the influence of the citation of this verse in Hebrews 2.7.

The examples discussed above are sufficient to illustrate the problems faced by any translator of the Psalms. In addition to matters requiring interpretation, however, there are also questions to be considered about the use for which the translation is required. In biblical translation generally the object is to produce as near as possible an equivalent in the receptor language to the original Hebrew, Aramaic or Greek text, in so far as that can be established and understood. Translations vary considerably in the degree of literalness. For instance, the KJV often reproduces the syntax of the original text, even though it is less natural in English. On the other hand some modern versions are much freer, but may be thought to convey the sense of the original text more clearly and intelligibly for an English readership. A translation of the Psalms for use in worship may properly be less literal than one intended for purposes of study, and may reasonably reflect the tradition of Christian interpretation. As we have seen in the case of the problems raised by inclusive language, it may also have to show sensitivity to the needs and susceptibilities of a modern congregation.

It is hardly surprising, then, that the version of the Psalms used in worship has often been different from the main version of the Bible in general use, including its use for the Scripture readings in services of worship. For instance, even Jerome's Gallican Psalter did not displace the old Roman Psalter in Roman Catholic worship in Italy until the 16th century, while his Hebrew Psalter never superseded his Gallican Psalter in the Vulgate or in liturgical use. In the Church of England the Psalter of the 'Great Bible', based on Miles Coverdale's translation from the Gallican Psalter of the Vulgate, remained in constant use in the BCP until the mid-20th century - for, though the Epistle and Gospel readings in the BCP were in 1662 put into the KJV, the Psalter remained that of the Great Bible. In fact the Coverdale Psalter remains in practically universal use to this day at choral evensong in cathedrals and college chapels where the Prayer Book rite is followed. The *Revised Psalter* of 1963 was an attempt to preserve as much as possible of the literary quality of Coverdale's Psalter, while making necessary adjustments to conform with the Hebrew text. What came to be known as the 'Liturgical Psalter' of 1977, which was incorporated into the ASB in 1980, was an ecumenical version made from the Hebrew text into modern English (including addressing God as 'you'). The Psalter in the CW main book of 2000 is an adaptation of that used in the Episcopal Church of the USA. All three of these Psalters from the second half of the 20th century were specifically designed for liturgical use. Differences between them reflect sometimes different judgements about what may have been the original Hebrew text, sometimes differences of interpretation, and sometimes differences in the style adopted for the particular translation (e.g. 'thou' or 'you' in the address to God, or the attitude to the questions posed by inclusive language). For scholarly study of the Psalms recourse must be had to the Hebrew text itself, but for their use in Christian worship the modern liturgical Psalters are generally sufficient, even if they cannot satisfy sophisticated individuals in every particular!

3. Use of the Psalms in Early Christian Worship

The Old Testament itself affords remarkably little direct indication of how and when the Psalms were used in the worship of Israel. For the most part we are left to make what inferences we can from the actual content of individual psalms. Occasionally, as in the case of Psalm 137, the content gives a clear indication of the occasion when a particular psalm was used. The title prefixed to Psalm 92, which, like all the titles, is secondary to the text of the psalm itself, indicates its use on the Sabbath, while that prefixed to Psalm 30 refers to the dedication of the house, presumably the Temple. The content of Psalm 30, however, suggests that this is a secondary use of a psalm originally intended as a thanksgiving for recovery from illness; perhaps the rededication of the Temple by Judas Maccabaeus after its desecration by Antiochus Epiphanes was thought of in this way.

Otherwise we gain only occasional glimpses of the use of psalms within the Old Testament. The refrain 'O give thanks to the LORD, for he is good; for his steadfast love endures for ever' (106.1, 107.1, 118.1, 136.1) is cited with reference to Temple worship at 2 Chronicles 5.13, and with particular reference to the restoration of worship after the exile at Jeremiah 33.11 and Ezra 3.11. In the account of the installation of the Ark in Jerusalem in 1 Chronicles 16 there is a pastiche of Psalms 105.1-15, 96.1-13a, the refrain cited above (106.1), and 106.47-48. These passages suggest that individual psalms were not necessarily always used as independent pieces, but may have been treated as a quarry of material for either shorter or longer liturgical compositions.

A major difficulty in accessing Jewish liturgical practice at the beginning of the Christian era is the fact that the main source, the Mishnah, did not reach its definitive form until the end of the second century. Although many of its contents are much earlier, the only criteria for dating specific traditions are references to Temple practice (which must predate the destruction of the Temple in 70), or sayings attributed to particular rabbis who can be dated at a specific time. Among the references to Temple practice *Tamid* 7.4 preserves a valuable record of the psalms which were sung in the Temple on the individual days of the week: 24 (Sunday), 48 (Monday), 82 (Tuesday), 94 (Wednesday), 81 (Thursday), 93 (Friday), and 92 (Sabbath). This practice was continued in the

Synagogue after the destruction of the Temple. Another ancient practice was the recitation of the group of Psalms known as the Hallel (113-118) at the Passover Seder, although *Pesahim* 10.6-7 records a difference between the schools of Shammai and Hillel over the point at which a break is made before the drinking of the third and fourth cups of wine. It is often thought that this is the hymn mentioned at the conclusion of the Last Supper in Mark 14.26, but the hymn is not identified, and it is by no means certain that the Last Supper was a formal Passover meal. *Sukkah* 3.1 and 4.5 refer specifically to the use of Psalm 118 at the feast of Tabernacles. The title of Psalm 29 in the Septuagint contains an additional element, a reference to its use at the end of Tabernacles, although there is no support for this in the Mishnah. Finally *Taanith* mentions the use of Psalms 120, 121, 130, and 102 at solemn fasts held at times of drought.

When we turn to the New Testament, specific evidence for the use of the Psalms in primitive Christian worship is again extremely sparse. There are general references to psalms in a context of public worship in 1 Corinthians 14.26, Ephesians 5.19, and Colossians 3.16, to which may be added James 5.13 in a context of private devotion. But it is far from certain that these references are specifically to the use of the canonical Psalter. Other references to the Psalms have a more apologetic purpose, treating them as scriptural authority for particular statements, e.g Luke 20.42-43, Acts 1.20, and 13.33. There is, however, an interesting and suggestive case in Acts 4.24-30, where a prayer of the primitive Christians is recorded, which includes a citation of Psalm 2.1-2.

Nor is there much specific evidence for the liturgical use of the Psalms in the first few Christian centuries. It is clear from patristic writings in general that the early Christians were thoroughly familiar with the Psalms, and it seems a reasonable inference that they were regularly used in early Christian communal worship, although many of the actual references probably refer simply to their use in personal private prayer. For details of which psalms were used on which occasions, however, there is very little evidence before the fourth century, and not a great deal even then.

An early reference to the use of psalms in corporate Christian worship is to be found in Tertullian, *De Oratione* 27. The practice is attributed to those who are more conscientious in praying, but Tertullian strongly recommends it. He says that they appended to their prayers 'Alleluia' and such kind of psalms that those present might respond with their endings. This tantalizingly brief and obscure reference leaves many questions unanswered, but does suggest that one person read the text of a psalm, while the congregation joined in an 'Alleluia' or other refrain. No specific psalms are mentioned, but Ps. 136, with its identical refrain in the second half of each verse, comes to mind as one which could easily be used in this way. Tertullian elsewhere refers to the specific use of Ps. 68 (in *Adversus Marcionem* 3.22), and Ps. 133 as suited to communal singing (in *De Jejunia* 13). In *De Anima* 9 he describes a Montanist service, including the reading of the scriptures, the singing of psalms, and the exhortation, but it is difficult to deduce any clear indication of the order of these elements, and in any case it refers to sectarian worship. Tertullian's account may be supplemented by the description of the liturgy used at the lighting of the lamp in *Apostolic Tradition* 25, which includes a mention of the reading of psalms by a deacon, with the congregation joining in with 'Alleluia'. The provenance and date of this work, which has widely been attributed to Hippolytus, have recently been brought into fresh discussion.

Eusebius records the dedication of churches after the cessation of persecution in his *Ecclesiastical History* 10.3, specifically mentioning the singing of psalms. In 10.4 he records the festival oration on the building of the churches, addressed to Paulinus, Bishop of Tyre. In the first part of this panegyric a number of verses from the psalms are quoted (44.1, 48.8, 87.3, 122.1, 26.8, and 48.1), and it may not be unreasonable to infer that these were among the psalms actually sung at the dedication services.

Athanasius in his *Letter to Marcellinus* seems to be concerned primarily with the use of the Psalms in individual private devotion. He does, however, encourage the singing rather than the mere recitation of psalms, and this probably reflects familiarity with their being sung in public worship. It is noteworthy, too, that he envisages the use of the whole Psalter, indicating how it covers the various situations and spiritual conditions in which an individual might seek an appropriate prayer. Furthermore he emphasizes the prophetic references to Christ in the Psalter as a whole, as well as indicating particular psalms relating to e.g. the incarnation, passion, resurrection, ascension, and second coming in judgement. At one point he confirms the appropriateness of particular psalms to four of the days of the week: 24 (Sunday), 95 (Monday), 94 (Wednesday), and 93 (Friday). It is interesting that three of these are in agreement with the Jewish practice cited at the beginning of this chapter, suggesting at least partial continuity with this practice in the early Church, although Athanasius gives somewhat tortuous Christological reasons for the Wednesday and Friday psalms. He also records a vigil service on Thursdays, which seems to have been peculiar to Alexandria, at which he says that Ps. 136.1 was one of the people's responses during the psalmody (*Defence of his Flight* 24).

Doubtless one of the reasons for the paucity of specific early evidence for the use of particular psalms on particular occasions, as of so many other details of early public Christian worship, is simply that everyone was familiar with the actual usage in their own worshipping community, so that no need was felt to record it. The *Pilgrimage of Egeria* is of special interest in this respect, since it contains considerable information about the daily services at the holy places in Jerusalem, reported for the information and interest of the members of Egeria's community at home. Psalms are clearly an integral and important part of these services. In her account of the service at the Lighting of the Lamps (24.4) she refers to the Lucernare psalms, and in that of the cock-crow service on Sunday mornings (24.9-11) she mentions three psalms at the beginning and a further psalm after the reading of the Gospel of the Resurrection. Unfortunately Egeria does not identify which psalms were used on any occasion, but she does say that the psalms were always appropriate to the time of day (25.5) or the liturgical day (25.10, referring to the Epiphany).

A few more specific details may be gleaned from Cyril of Jerusalem. In his *Procatechesis* 15 he encourages those who have been enrolled for the forthcoming Easter baptism to look forward to hearing the angelic choirs singing Ps. 32.1 as they enter the church from their baptism. It is not unreasonable to suppose that this psalm was actually used at this point in the baptismal liturgy at Jerusalem. In the *Mystagogical Lectures* ascribed to Cyril there are specific references to the use of Ps. 26.6 at the Lavabo, and of Ps. 34.8 at the reception of communion in the Easter eucharist (5.2,20). The use of this psalm at the reception of communion is mentioned also in *Apostolic Constitutions* 8.13.

Chrysostom too makes a few references to the use of particular psalms. For instance he indicates that Ps. 145.15 was used as a refrain by initiates (*Expositio in Ps. 144* 1), from which it seems probable that the psalm itself was used at the Communion. He also makes it quite clear that Ps. 141 was used as the daily evening psalm (see v. 2) and Ps. 63 as the morning psalm (*Expositio in Ps. 140*.1), a usage which is confirmed by *Apostolic Constitutions* 2.59. Elsewhere he refers to the use of Ps. 134.2 and Ps. 148.1 during the service at cock-crow (*Homily 14 on 1 Timothy*

4). Occasionally he identifies a particular verse of a psalm as that repeated by the congregation as a refrain during the rendering of the psalm as a whole. Thus he specifies v. 1 as the refrain for Ps. 42 (*Expositio in Ps 41.* 5), and v. 24 as that for Ps. 118 (*Expositio in Ps. 117*).

Augustine gives us tantalizing glimpses of the use of psalmody in the eucharist in his day. He was evidently accustomed to preach on the Scriptures used on the particular occasion, and most of the information he provides has to be gleaned from his extant sermons. The Psalm always came between the Epistle and the Gospel, with an Old Testament reading sometimes preceding the Epistle, and the sermon following the Gospel. Often, although not always, the choice of the readings was at the bishop's discretion, and Augustine often chose a passage to suit the subject of his intended sermon. On one occasion, for instance, he selected the Epistle reading to fit the psalm which had been sung and on which he wished to preach. On another occasion he chose a short psalm, but the lector mistakenly sang Ps. 139 in its place, whereupon Augustine changed his topic and preached on this psalm instead! On yet another occasion the use of Psalm 51 led Augustine to preach on repentance.[1]

Augustine also mentions the singing of psalms at both the offertory and the communion, the former practice having been introduced at Hippo in his own time, against some opposition (*Retractiones* 2.11). Furthermore he provides some information about the use of particular psalms at certain occasions, such as Ps. 85 at Christmas, Ps. 22 on Good Friday, Ps. 118 at Easter (attested also in the paschal homily of an ancient author), Ps. 19 at the Feast of Ss. Peter and Paul, and Ps. 30 at the Consecration of a Church (compare the title prefixed to this psalm in the Hebrew Bible and the Septuagint). On the use of the psalms he insists that the meaning of the words is more important than the music of the singing, although he recognizes that weaker minds may be stirred to devotion through the beauty of the music (*Confessions* 10.33).It is interesting that in this same passage he refers to Athanasius having required so slight an inflection of the voice of the reader of the psalm that it was more like speaking than singing. Theologically Augustine maintains that in the psalms it is Christ who is praying in the Church: 'when the body of the Son prays it does not separate its head from itself' (*Commentary on Ps. 85* 1[2]).

---

[1] See G. G. Willis, *St. Augustine's Lectionary* (Alcuin Club Collection 44, SPCK, 1966) pp. 7-8 for references and further details.

[2] This is conveniently accessible as the reading for the Saturday after Epiphany 1 in Robert Atwell (ed), *Celebrating the Seasons* (Canterbury Press, 1999) pp. 84-5.

From the second half of the fourth century much more detailed information becomes available, and in the remainder of this chapter it will be convenient to treat the liturgical use of the Psalms thematically rather than chronologically. It will be possible within the confines of the present work only to indicate the broad outlines of the development of liturgical practice, and the emphasis will be chiefly on the West.

The earliest and most consistent point at which psalmody has been used in the eucharist is in the Liturgy of the Word, where it has functioned as an integral element of the Scriptural material, a reading in its own right even when sung, and one on which a sermon might be based as much as on any other reading. The number of readings and the relative position of the psalmody varied from place to place, but the evidence suggests that the psalm was most commonly located just before the Gospel reading. We have seen how the use of specific psalms on particular occasions was only beginning to come into force in Augustine's time. We have already noted the early evidence for a psalm at the distribution of communion, and for the introduction of a psalm at the offertory at Hippo in Augustine's time.

The last point at which psalmody seems to have been introduced into the eucharist was at the Introit. There is no precise evidence for the introduction of this usage, but the detailed instructions in *Ordo Romanus I* indicate that by the eighth century only as much of the psalm was sung as was required to cover the entry of the papal procession. It was introduced by an antiphon, which was then repeated after each verse of the psalm, until the Pope gave the signal for the psalm to be concluded with the *Gloria Patri* and a final repetition of the antiphon. In the course of time in the Western eucharist the individual portions of psalmody came to be much reduced, in the case of the Introit to a single verse in addition to the antiphon, while in that at the distribution of communion only the antiphon survived. Mention should also be made of the use of psalmody in the ancillary devotions to the eucharist, of which perhaps the best known example is the use of Ps. 43 (where v. 4 has an obvious relevance) in the priest's immediate preparation to celebrate the Eecharist.

There can be no doubt that the liturgical context where the psalms have been most intensively used is that of the daily services of praise and prayer. The origins and early development of these services remain in many ways obscure, and their subsequent development is far too complex to consider in any detail in the present work. Modern study of these services has been dominated by the distinction made by Anton Baumstark[3] between what he called a 'Cathedral Rite' and a 'Monastic Rite'. The first of these were public services, attended by laity as well as clergy; the second were a parallel development within the monastic movement. In the course of time the Monastic Rite gained a growing influence over the Cathedral Rite, so that the actual secular offices became a hybrid form with a strongly monastic flavour.

It is in the use of psalmody that the two kinds of office are most sharply distinguished. The *Pilgrimage of Egeria* is one of the earliest sources for the Cathedral Rite, and it is interesting that Egeria mentions additional devotions of the '*monazontes*' and '*parthenae*' before the arrival of the bishop with his clergy for the Cathedral office (24.1). Her account of the latter makes it clear that it includes a substantial use of psalmody, always appropriate to the time of day or the liturgical season, although unfortunately she does not specify which particular psalms were used. Numerous sources indicate Ps. 63 as a regular morning psalm and Ps. 141 as a regular evening psalm, as we have already seen from Chrysostom. This information can be supplemented from other sources. Basil (Letter 207.3) mentions the use of the psalm of confession (51) at the beginning of the Cathedral morning office. Caesarius of Arles (Sermon 136.1) refers to the widespread use of Ps. 104 at the evening office.

The Monastic Rite, on the other hand, grew out of the concept of the spiritual training and development of the individual monk, with the ideal of 'prayer without ceasing', in which the use of the whole Psalter was from the earliest times the norm. The particular schemes for the use of the Psalter varied from place to place, particularly in the quantity of psalmody used on each occasion, and the period of time over which the whole Psalter was used. What was consistent, however, was the comprehensive use of all the psalms, in strict numerical order, without regard to appropriateness to the time of day or the liturgical season.

John Cassian is one of the earliest witnesses to this monastic usage. He records how the monks in Lower Egypt engaged in manual labour throughout the day in their cells, accompanied by 'prayer without ceasing', coming together for a corporate act of worship only twice, in the evening and for the night vigil (*Institutes* 3.2). He mentions the use of twelve psalms at both the evening and the nocturnal services. But he stresses the

---

[3]   A Baumstark, *Comparative Liturgy* (English Edition by F. L. Cross, Mowbray, 1958) pp. 111-2.

meditative approach even there, each psalm or portion of a psalm being followed by a period of silent prayer and then a vocal prayer before proceeding to the next. He also mentions the use of the *Gloria Patri* at the end of the psalmody, noting, however, that this was not the practice in the East (*Institutes* 2.5-8). Cassian also distinguishes three different ways of rendering the psalms. Sometimes a single cantor sang the psalm, while the congregation listened (*Institutes* 2.10-12). At other times either two choirs sang alternately (the antiphonal method) (*Institutes* 2.2), or the congregation contributed an intermittent response, while a single voice rendered the text of the psalm (the responsorial method)(*Institutes* 3.8.4).

In addition to the details given above there is sporadic evidence for the use of particular psalms at particular times. In addition to Ps. 63 the *Ordo Monasterii* 2 mentions the use of Pss. 5 and 90 at Mattins, and Basil (*Longer Rule* 37.2-5) confirms this use of Ps.5. Cassian mentions the use of Pss. 148-150 at the end of the night vigil at Bethlehem (*Institutes* 3.6). These psalms certainly came very widely in time to form the climax of the morning office. For instance Arnobius the Younger, an African monk living in Rome in the fifth century, says in his *Commentary on Ps. 148* that this psalm was sung at dawn throughout the world. The *Rule of the Master* 32.14 mentions the use of Ps. 95 as an invitatory psalm at the beginning of Nocturns. Basil mentions the use of Ps. 91 at both the midday service and Compline (*Longer Rule* 37.3-5), no doubt in view of the double application of v.6. He also mentions the use of Ps. 55 (see v. 17) at midday, and of Pss. 51 and 143 at the third hour. In his *Exposition of Ps. 118* (i.e. 119) 19:30,32 Ambrose alludes to Pss. 65.8 and 119.148 in such a way as to suggest that they formed part of the morning office. Finally Aurelian gives us a rare glimpse of psalmody proper to the season when he records the use on alternate days in Easter week of Ps. 68.33-6 and Ps. 113.1-3 as invitatories at the evening office (*Rule for Monks* 56.7-8).[4]

In the course of time in both East and West hybrid forms of the office evolved, with both cathedral and monastic features. The most prominent monastic feature was the use of the whole psalter, while cathedral influence persisted in the use of certain fixed psalms. In the Byzantine office, for instance, there was a set of six psalms (3, 38, 63, 88, 103, and 143) used at both Mattins and Compline. Other psalms used in the morning office included 20, 21, 119, 135 + 136, 51, and 148-150. The invitatory at the evening office was 104, and other fixed psalms were 141,

---

[4]   See R. Taft, *The Liturgy of the Hours in East and West*, p. 111 for a discussion of the extent of these invitatories.

142, 130, and 117. For the continuous use of the Psalter the psalms were divided into twenty *kathismata*, each consisting of three *staseis*. These were used in varying groups and varying quantities at the morning and evening offices, the whole Psalter generally being recited in the course of a week.

In the West the Rule of Benedict became particularly influential. Benedict (*Rule* 18) lamented that the Fathers used to recite the whole Psalter every day, but resolved that his community should do it at least once a week. The details are set out in *Rule* 9-18. Pss. 1-20 are used at Prime, 21-109 at Mattins or Nocturns, 110-118 and 129-147 at Vespers, while 119-128 are used at Terce, Sext, and None. Special psalms are used at Lauds (67, 51, two variable psalms, and 148-150) and Compline (4, 91, and 134). Psalms 3 and 95 are used as invitatories at the beginning of the night office.

Another significant detail in Benedict's *Rule* is the specification of particular psalm verses to be used as versicles at the beginning of offices: Ps. 51.15 at the night office and Ps. 70.1 at the others. Cassian (*Conferences* 10.10[5]) recommended the use of the latter at all times as a focus of continual prayer and meditation. Michael Perham draws out the significance of these two versicles as expressing the balance between the giving of praise and the receiving of grace in his lecture 'Benedict and the Worship of the Church Today'.[6] Ps. 85.4 was later added as the opening versicle at Compline.

Before leaving the topic of the daily services a brief mention should be made of Cardinal Quiñones' abortive reformed Breviary in two editions of 1535 and 1536, in view of its influence on Cranmer's work of producing the first Book of Common Prayer in 1549. By this time the use of proper psalms for saints' days, and of additional groups of psalms such as the gradual psalms (120-134) and the penitential psalms (6, 32, 38, 51, 102, 130, 143) on a daily basis, had seriously disrupted the weekly recitation of the whole Psalter. This Quiñones restored with a scheme that allotted three psalms to each office for eight offices a day, spread over the seven days of the week, the allocation to each office being invariable. The psalms did not, however, follow the numerical order.

---

[5] This is conveniently accessible as the reading for the Friday after Lent 2 in Robert Atwell (ed), *Celebrating the Seasons*, pp. 172-3. A further reading on praying the psalms from *Conferences* 10.11 may be found for the Monday after Trinity 5, pp. 346-7.

[6] This lecture was given at the Annual General Meeting of the Alcuin Club on 9 May 2006, and was subsequently printed and circulated among the membership. See pp.3-5 for the specific reference.

We turn finally to some of the early evidence for the use of psalms at the occasional services. We have already noted the mention of Ps. 32 in connection with baptism in the *Procatechesis* of Cyril of Jerusalem. Ps. 51 seems also to have been widely used at baptism in the Eastern churches. The Armenian Rite prescribes Pss. 25, 26, and 51 at the beginning of the service, Ps. 118.1-19 after the Creed, Pss. 29 and 23 at the blessing of the water, Ps. 34 after the baptism itself, and Ps. 32 as the newly baptized are escorted out of the church at the end of the service[7]. In the West Ps. 42 seems to be the most widely attested psalm at baptism, being mentioned specifically in the *Gelasian Sacramentary* (XLIII) as used with an accompanying collect at the end of the series of readings at the Easter vigil, followed immediately by the procession to the font.

With regard to the marriage service Gregory of Nazianzus quotes Ps. 128.5 in the context of a prayer of blessing.[8] This psalm appears in the Byzantine marriage rite in the tenth century[9], and in the Sarum, York, and Hereford Manuals between the marriage ceremony itself and the nuptial mass that follows.[10] Other psalms sometimes used in the Eastern marriage rites include 19 (see v5), 21, and 45 (compare the royal overtones of the 'coronation' of the couple in the Eastern tradition).[11]

The psalm most frequently used in the funeral service seems to be 116 (see v15). This is mentioned specifically in *Apostolic Constitutions* 6.30, and also, together with Pss. 23 and 32, by Chrysostom (*Homily on Hebrews* 4.7). Augustine's account of his mother Monica's funeral includes Ps. 101 (*Confessions* ix, 12). The Byzantine funeral rite includes Pss. 91 and 119 during the procession to the church, and Ps. 51 during the service there, while Pss. 23, 24, and 84 were used at a priest's funeral.[12] The Gelasian funeral rite includes Pss. 116 and 143 during the procession to the church.[13]

Ps. 132 was widely used in the Eastern churches at the ordination of higher ranks of the clergy (see v.9). Not surprisingly this psalm, together with Ps. 24.7-10 and other psalms, was also used at the consecration of

---

[7]   E. C. Whitaker, *Documents of the Baptismal Liturgy* (2nd edn, SPCK, 1970) pp. 61-6.
[8]   K. Stevenson, *Nuptial Blessing* (ACC 64, Alcuin/SPCK, 1982) p. 22.
[9]   ib., p. 98.
[10] ib. p. 80.
[11] J. A. Lamb, *The Psalms in Christian Worship* (Faith Press, 1962) p. 73.
[12] G. Rowell, *The Liturgy of Christian Burial* (ACC 59, Mayhew/McCrimmon, 1977) pp. 32-35.
[13] ib., p. 58.

churches.[14] In the Western church ordinations took place within the eucharist, and the psalmody used was that of the eucharist[15]. A number of psalms were used at the consecration of churches, mostly in conjunction with particular ceremonies, e.g. Ps. 24 at the arrival of the bishop at the church door, and Ps. 43 at the anointing of the altar.[16] In general it may be observed that the psalms selected for use at the occasional services have an obvious relevance to the particular rite in which they are used, and thus the characteristic of appropriateness noted already by Egeria remained a guiding principle.

[14]   Lamb, *op. cit.*, pp. 77-78.
[15]   ib., p. 126.
[16]   ib., p. 127.

4. Use of the Psalms in the Church of England

Although the Church of England is continuous with the Church in this country from at least the third century, its distinctive liturgical history begins effectively with the appearance of the first Book of Common Prayer in 1549. Although this Book was superseded in turn by a radical revision in 1552 and more modest revisions in 1559 and 1662, the 1549 Prayer Book has in itself and through these changes had a formative and lasting influence on worship in the Church of England and in the wider Anglican Communion. In England itself the 1662 Prayer Book remained the only authorized liturgy until 1966, although many of the provisions of the Proposed Prayer Book of 1928, which was never authorized, were widely used between then and 1966. The period of authorized experiment initiated in 1966 reached a first climax in the ASB of 1980, which in turn was superseded by the Common Worship series (no longer a single book) from 2000. Considerations of space preclude any survey of the various Prayer Books of other churches of the Anglican Communion. In practice the present Study is concerned chiefly with the books of 1549, 1552, 1662, 1928, 1980 and 2000, and it will be convenient to refer to them simply by these dates.

The Preface of the 1549 Prayer Book, which appears in the 1662 Book under the heading 'Concerning the Service of the Church', sets out a number of principles by which the Anglican liturgy was to be reformed. Two of these are of immediate relevance for the Psalter. One is the principle that Scripture should be read as a whole, and the other that the practical arrangement should be simple and straightforward. The pattern of daily services was reduced from eight to two services, and the Psalms were to be read in strict numerical order. The Psalter was divided into 60 portions, only one psalm (119) being divided over more than one portion. The 60 portions were to be read, two a day, over the thirty days of a calendar month. Since February has only 28 days, it was to "borrow" one each from January and March. In the remaining months with 31 days, the psalms for the 30th day were to be repeated on the last day. This pattern was interrupted on only four occasions in the year, when proper psalms were provided for the major festivals: Christmas Day, Easter Day, Ascension Day, and Whitsunday (Pentecost). In 1549 these provisions, together with a more extensive set of proper Scripture readings, were given in conjunction with the Collects and Readings for use at Holy Communion. In 1552 these provisions for Morning and Evening Prayer were abstracted, and appended as a Table attached to the introductory sections on the Orders for reading the Psalter and the rest of Holy Scripture. To these four days Ash Wednesday and Good Friday were added in 1662. This scheme certainly achieved the two ideals of comprehensiveness and simplicity, but at the cost of minimal appropriateness to the liturgical season or the time of day. Most of the psalms particularly appropriate to the evening (4, 31, 91, 134, and 141) fell into portions appointed to be read at the morning service, only Ps. 104 being assigned to the evening. The Gloria Patri was to be used at the end of every psalm and canticle except the Te Deum.

A further detail in the provisions of the 1549 book may conveniently be noted here. To the Collects, Epistles and Gospels appointed for each Sunday and holy day was prefixed an Introit Psalm for use at the beginning of Holy Communion. The selection of psalms seems to have been made by a mixture of two procedures. First, psalms suitable for the occasion were chosen wherever possible, and then short psalms in numerical order were selected to fill the gaps.[17] These Introit Psalms disappeared in 1552, and have never been replaced in subsequent BCPs.

In addition to the use of Psalmody in numerical order, or occasional proper psalms, in the daily services, we should note the unvarying use of Ps. 95 as an invitatory before the psalms of the day at Matins in 1549, replaced only by the Easter Anthems on Easter Day in 1552. The 1552 book introduced a further provision of specific psalms as alternatives to the Gospel canticles at Morning and Evening Prayer: the Benedictus (Ps.100), Magnificat (Ps. 98), and Nunc Dimittis (Ps. 67). No psalm alternatives, however, were provided for the first canticle at Morning Prayer, which remained either the Te Deum or the Benedicite from the Apocrypha.

Some, mostly small but significant, changes were introduced in the 1928 book. The Venite (Ps. 95) at Morning Prayer was shortened to the first seven verses, and made optional except on Sundays and holy days. An optional invitatory antiphon was also provided for the main seasons and holy days, although it was not widely used. It consisted of a single sentence or phrase, followed by 'O come, let us adore him, (Alleluia)', and was to be used once before the Venite and again after its closing Gloria Patri. The only modification to the psalms appointed as alternatives to the

---

[17] F. E. Brightman, *The English Rite*, vol. I, p. xciv; G. Cuming, *The Godly Order* (ACC 65, Alcuin/SPCK, 1983) p. 63.

canticles was the addition of 51 (or 40, if 51 had already been used) in place of the first canticle at Morning Prayer. Although this is not stated, its use as an alternative during Lent seems to have been in mind.

In the monthly cycle Pss. 113 and 141 could be transferred optionally from morning to evening on their respective days. In both cases the main object seems to have been to achieve a more even balance of quantity between the two services, although the reference to the evening sacrifice in Ps. 141 may well have been an additional factor. For the first time permission was given to omit certain verses, and in one case a whole psalm (58), because they were felt to be inconsistent with the New Testament ethic. The 'cursing psalms' had long been a problem, and ingenious methods of reinterpretation had been adopted to sanitize them, but this was the first time that the principle of the comprehensive use of the whole Psalter was breached.

Undoubtedly the most significant development in the 1928 book was the considerable extension of the provision of proper psalms. In the new table 'one or more of the appointed psalms' might be used at the Minister's discretion in place of the psalms of the monthly cycle. Proper psalms were now provided for every Sunday, for the Circumcision and Epiphany, and for each day in Holy Week, while lists of suitable psalms were provided as a kind of pool for holy days, Rogation days, Dedication and Harvest Festivals, and a few other occasions. In addition to the much wider provision of proper psalms the element of local discretion must be noted. At the same time there was no general seasonal provision. If, for instance, Easter Day fell on 3 April, Ps. 22 would still be used on the evening of Easter Monday! It is also a little surprising that no provision was made in the 1928 book for the use of psalmody at Holy Communion.

In the ASB of 1980 psalms at Morning and Evening Prayer could continue to be used according to the monthly cycle as in the 1662 book, together with the proper psalms on the six occasions provided there. The main provision, however, is included with the Scripture readings in the lectionary tables, covering both Sundays and holy days, when the selection is thematic, and weekdays, when it follows a sequential pattern spread over just under ten weeks. Clearly the average amount of psalmody per weekday service is considerably less than in the monthly cycle. A number of the longer psalms (18, 37, 78, 89, 105, 106, and 107) are divided over two services, while Ps. 119 is divided over nine (as opposed to five in the monthly cycle). Pss. 58 and 109 might be omitted in their entirety, while certain verses of other psalms are bracketed for optional omission, as in 1928. One advantage of this arrangement in comparison with the monthly cycle is that the sequence is not interrupted every week by the proper psalms on Sundays, although it is of course interrupted by proper psalms on holy days occurring on fixed calendar dates; this sometimes had the unfortunate effect that only one half of a divided psalm was used.

There were also several changes in the use of fixed psalms within the services. The invitatory psalm at Morning Prayer continued to be the Venite, but this was now modified to consist of Ps. 95.1-7 + Ps. 96.10. Ps. 100, as well as the Easter Anthems, was now provided as an alternative invitatory, and is clearly much more appropriate at that point in the service (see verses 2 and 4) than as an alternative to the canticle after the second Scripture reading. Another innovation was the provision of an optional parallel invitatory before the psalms at Evening Prayer, consisting of Ps. 134, the hymn 'O gladsome light', or the Easter Anthems. No mention is made of the use of psalms as alternatives to the Gospel canticles. The most significant change in the 1980 book, however, is undoubtedly the provision of two psalms or portions of psalms with each set of readings for Sundays and holy days at Holy Communion. The precise position of these psalms within the service was not prescribed, but the rubrics indicate that they might be used as an introit at the beginning of the service (as in 1549), or between either the Old Testament and New Testament readings, or the New Testament and Gospel readings. In practice rarely more than one piece of psalmody was used, and generally between the readings rather than as an introit. The provision of psalmody at Holy Communion was, however, a recognition of its central importance in Christian worship, as well of the fact that by this time Holy Communion was the only service attended regularly by many churchgoers.

With the publication of the main Common Worship volume in 2000, and the definitive edition of *Common Worship: Daily Prayer* in 2005, we reach the current liturgical provision in the Church of England. The Calendar and Lectionary in the former covers only Sundays and Holy Days, but the provision is in each cases for three services, designated respectively the Principal Service, Second Service, and Third Service. These would normally be Holy Communion, and Morning and Evening Prayer or some other 'Service of the Word', but the provision could be distributed in different ways between these services, to allow for variation in the weekly pattern of services, while preserving continuity in the lectionary followed at whatever service was used at a particular time.

Psalmody is provided for each of these services, although only one portion, often only part of a psalm, is provided for the Principal Service, where its use as a gradual between the readings is clearly envisaged as the norm. One noteworthy feature of the provisions for 'A Service of the Word', which includes less formal 'family services' as well as Morning and Evening Prayer, Prayer During the Day and Night Prayer, is the note that *'The service should normally include a psalm or psalms'* (p. 27, n. 6). Although a metrical version may be used, or a psalm *'occasionally be replaced by a ... scriptural song'*, this instruction clearly recognizes the importance of psalmody and promotes its use. To what extent this is being observed in practice, particularly in less formal services, is an interesting question.

The provision of psalmody at weekday services is more complex, and is to be found partly in *Daily Prayer* and partly in the CW *Weekday Lectionary*, authorized in 2005, of which the definitive publication appeared in February 2008. For Morning and Evening Prayer Psalm Tables are provided for each of the seasons of Advent, Christmas, Epiphany, Lent, Easter, and the period from All Saints to the Eve of Advent. The psalms are selected with a view to giving an appropriate seasonal flavour to the services, and distributed among the days and weeks of each season in such a way that the same psalm does not occur at the same service each week within the season (with an eye to college chapels or churches where there may be a regular choral evensong on a particular day of the week). During ordinary time a similar table is provided, extending over seven weeks. Ps. 119 is used in sections of 24 or 32 verses on Wednesdays, alternately in the morning and evening. Otherwise the psalms are followed in approximately numerical order, with some minor adjustments to ensure the use of evening psalms at Evening Prayer, psalms with a Passion flavour on Fridays, and an equitable distribution of the length of psalmody at each service. Duplicated psalms (e.g. 14 and 53) are used only once, and Psalms 58, 83 and 109 are omitted entirely. This table may be used in place of the seasonal tables except between 19 December and Epiphany and during Holy Week and Easter Week. For those who prefer a strictly numerical course the monthly pattern as modified in the 1928 book is provided as an alternative table. One further innovation in the CW *Daily Prayer* Psalter is the provision of optional refrains or antiphons for use at the beginning and end (after the Gloria) of each psalm, except in a few cases like Ps. 46, where certain verses within the psalm are already indicated as constituting possible refrains. Another provision is that of an optional short prayer which may be used after a period of silence in place of the Gloria at the end of the psalm.

In addition to Morning and Evening Prayer CW *Daily Prayer* also makes provision for two further offices, either of which may be used either independently or in conjunction with Morning and Evening Prayer. One is 'Prayer During the Day', which is intended primarily as a short midday office, but which can be used at any time, particularly envisaging some for whom this will be their only opportunity to partake in the cycle of Daily Prayer. Two tables using Pss. 119 and 121-133 over a week, a fortnight, or a month, are provided; these are designed particularly when this office is used in addition to Morning and Evening Prayer. Otherwise a four-week cycle is provided for use in ordinary time, and a weekly cycle for use during each of the seasons. For the other office, 'Night Prayer', one or more of the evening psalms 4, 91 and 134 may be used on any day, while alternatives are also provided for the days of the week and the seasons.

CW *Daily Prayer* does not use psalms as alternatives to canticles, but it does offer a wider selection of invitatory psalms for optional use as part of the Preparation at Morning and Evening Prayer. 18 psalms or parts of psalms are used in this way, and they are conveniently printed as a group of Psalm Canticles on pp. 551-568. These are Pss. 8, 18, 24, 27, 42, 51, 63, 67, 85, 95, 96, 100, 103 (two selections), 104, 134, 141, and 143.

When we turn to the occasional services we find no use of psalmody in Baptism, Confirmation or the services of the Ordinal (which first appeared in 1552) before the ASB of 1980. In the Churching of Women, however, the 1549 and 1552 books prescribe Ps. 121, but this is replaced by Pss. 116 or 127 in the 1662 and 1928 books. This service is replaced by those of Thanksgiving for the Birth of a Child and of Thanksgiving after Adoption in the ASB, both of which include the optional use of Ps. 100. In the definitive edition of CW *Christian Initiation* (2006) the only provision for psalmody in the single service of Thanksgiving for a Child is the inclusion of Pss. 20, 128, and 139:7-18 among a list of suitable Bible Readings which may be used. Psalms are also suggested for use in the orders for the Presentation of each of the Four Texts (Jesus' Summary of the Law, the Lord's Prayer, the Apostles' Creed, and the Beatitudes) for adult converts preparing for Baptism over a period.

Provision is made for psalmody within the Liturgy of the Word at Baptism and/or Confirmation within the Eucharist or Morning or Evening Prayer in the ASB. The main suggestions are Ps. 107.1-9 and 121, with the following allowed as alternatives: 18.32-39, 25.1-10, 27.1-8, 34.1-8, and 97.9-end. Similar provisions are made in *Common Worship: Initiation*

Services. Apart from separate lists for use with a seasonal emphasis, psalms suggested for use at Baptism are: 66.4-11, 89.21-22 + 25-29, 51.1-7, and 46.1-7. Psalms for use at Confirmation are: 51.7-14 or 84.1-6, while at a Confirmation when Affirmation and Reception take place 18.31-38 and 107.1-9 are suggested. In each case the psalm belongs to a particular group of readings. One further provision in these services is the use of Ps. 42.1-7 among several canticles and litanies that may be used during the Procession to the Font.

CW *Christian Initiation* also includes a Corporate Service of Penitence, for which a table of readings including psalms for a number of different occasions is provided.This may be compared with the Commination Service for Ash Wednesday in all the Prayer Books from 1549 to 1662, which includes Ps. 51, while the similar service entitled 'Exhortation' in the Appendix of 1928 uses Ps. 130. In CW *Christian Initiation* there are also forms of service for the Reconciliation of a Penitent, which make use of selections of verses from several psalms. The service for a Celebration of Wholeness and Healing includes a table of psalms and readings for use on a variety of occasions.

The Ordinal in the ASB provides a psalm for use during the Liturgy of the Word: 119.33-38 at the ordination of deacons, 145.1-7 + 21 at that of priests, or or deacons and priests together, and 119:165-174 at that of a bishop. In CW *Ordination Services* (2007) the following psalms are recommended as 'particularly appropriate' for the several orders: 86.1-5 + 11-12, 113, and 119.1-5 for deacons, 99, 103.17-end, 118.19-26, 119.33-40. and 145.1-7 +22 for priests/presbyters, and 40.1-14, 99 and 100 for bishops.

In Matrimony Pss. 128 and 67 are appointed as alternatives in the 1549, 1552 and 1662 books, while a third alternative, Ps. 37.3-7, is provided in 1928. In the ASB the psalms provided are 67, 121 or 128, to which 127 is added in CW *Pastoral Services* (2000). In both of these books a hymn is allowed as an alternative to the psalm, while both are optional in the CW service. A suggestive difference may be noted in the rubrics of these two orders. In the ASB the rubric reads: '*One or more of the following PSALMS are used, or A HYMN may be sung*'. In the CW service the rubric is simply '*A hymn or psalm may be used*', with a reference to the pages where the psalms are printed. This probably reflects the decline in the use of psalms at weddings within the 20 years separating the publication of the two orders of service.

In the Visitation of the Sick Pss. 143 and 71 are provided in 1549, together with Ps. 13 after the administration of Unction, and Ps. 117 as the Introit at the Communion of the Sick. In 1552 and 1662 only Ps. 71 remains, while in 1928 it is replaced by Ps. 121. In 1928 a note is appended to the order for the Visitation, listing prayers and Scriptural passages suitable for use in pastoral ministry to the sick. This list includes a number of other psalms, but their use in this context is hardly liturgical. The ASB did not include provision for ministry to the sick, but separate provisions were published later: *Ministry to the Sick* in 1983, and *Ministry at the Time of Death* in 1991. The first of these includes Pss. 23, 46, 121, and verses from Pss. 91 and 145, while the second includes only Ps. 23. In CW *Pastoral Services* Ps.20.1-4 and responsories based on Pss. 91 and 121 are provided for the *Ministry to the Sick*, and Pss. 23 and 139 for *Ministry at the Time of Death*.

The greatest variety is to be found in the provision of the several orders for the Burial Service. 1549 appoints Pss. 116, 139 and 146, together with Ps. 42 as the Introit at Holy Communion on the occasion of a burial. No psalms at all are appointed in 1552, while 1662 appoints Pss. 39 and/or 90, to which 1928 adds Pss. 23 and 130. Ps. 23 alone is provided for the new service for the Burial of a Child in 1928. This book also allows the use of part of Ps. 103 (vv. 13-17) as an alternative to the anthems beginning 'Man that is born of a woman' in the immediate prelude to the interment. Slightly different selections from this psalm are provided at this point in the ASB and CW services. In the main funeral service the psalms appointed in the ASB are 23, verses from 90, 121 and 130, to which 27, 42.1-7, verses from 118 or verses from 139 may be used as alternatives. At the funeral of a child only Ps. 23 is appointed. In CW the psalms listed for use are 6, 23, 25, 27, 32, 38.9-end, 42, 90, 116, 118.4-end, 121 and 139, while a section containing prayers for use after certain psalms includes the following further psalms by implication: 39, 120, 130, and 138. At the funeral of a child the choice is between Pss. 23 and 84.1-4.

Both the ASB and CW *Pastoral Services* contain provision for services additional to the main funeral service. Both contain a service for use before a funeral, in which the psalms provided are 27.1-8 and 139.1-11 + 17-18 in the ASB, and 121 in CW. CW also provides for a vigil before a funeral, with a whole set of different readings with psalms under a variety of themes. The ASB includes prayers for use after the birth of a still-born child or the death of a newly-born child, of which one is a pastiche of verses from several psalms, to which the following psalms may be used as alternatives: 23, 31:1-6, 103.8 + 13-17, 130, 139.1-9, and 142.1-6. CW also provides Pss. 71.1-6 + 17-18, 126.5-6 or 139.7-11 for use at a service after a funeral, and Pss. 16.4-10, 90.1-4 or 139.1-11 + 13 at a service for the burial of ashes. A comparison of the selection of psalmody used in connection with dying, death and funeral rites with changes in the perception and nature of such rites would make an interesting study, but would take us beyond the scope of this booklet.

In addition to the formal use of psalms or portions of psalms account must be taken of the use of material from the Psalter in other parts of the services. Verses of psalms are to be found among collections of Scripture Sentences found at several points, e.g. in the penitential sentences at the beginning of Morning and Evening Prayer or the offertory sentences in the 1662 order for Holy Communion, or among the Introductory and Post-communion Sentences provided with the Collects and Readings in the ASB of 1980.

Here we must note in particular the use of single verses of a psalm to provide a versicle and response as part of a dialogue between the leader and congregation. The most obvious examples of this are the use of Ps. 51.15 and Ps. 70.1 before the psalmody in Morning and Evening Prayer. The CW orders have reverted to the practice of the medieval western church in using the first at Morning Prayer and the second at Evening Prayer, but Cranmer combined both at Matins in 1549, and at Evening Prayer in 1552, and they remained in joint use until the ASB of 1980. Further examples of this may be seen in the set of six versicles and responses between the Lord's Prayer and the Collects in Morning and Evening Prayer in the Prayer Books from 1549 to 1928 (modified only slightly in the ASB of 1980). Of these the first is from Ps. 85.7, the second from Ps. 20.9, the third from Ps. 132.9, the fourth from Ps. 28.9a, and the sixth from Ps. 51.10a + 11b. Only the fifth is not a direct quotation from a psalm.

A slightly more elaborate use of verses from psalms may be found in the slightly varying forms of responsories. An example may be found in the Prayer Books from 1549 to 1662 in the prayers at the end of the Litany. The opening verse of Ps. 44 is preceded and followed by a slightly varying refrain based on the last verse of the psalm, the whole being completed by the *Gloria Patri*. In the 1928 the pattern is completed by the repetition of the refrain in its first form after the *Gloria Patri*. The Order for Compline in 1928 provides another example derived entirely from Ps. 31.6. The first half of the verse is said first by the leader and then by the congregation. The leader then says the second half of the verse, and the congregation the clause 'I commend my spirit'. Finally the leader says the first half of the *Gloria Patri*, after which the congregation repeats the first half of the psalm verse. CW *Daily Prayer* provides a number of responsories on this pattern, some of which use material from the psalms. An example may be seen in the orders for Morning and Evening Prayer on Wednesdays in ordinary time, using vv. 23 and 24 of Ps. 73. The leader says v. 24, and the congregation repeats it. The leader then says v. 23, after which the congregation repeats the second half of v. 24. The leader then says the first half of the *Gloria Patri*, after which the congregation repeats v. 24.

This may be considered also with relation to the provision of optional refrains for use with the Psalms in CW *Daily Prayer*. These often, but not always, consist of one particular verse or part of a verse of a psalm, as in the case of Ps. 1, where the refrain consists of the first half of the last verse. These are intended for use at the beginning of the psalm and again after the closing *Gloria Patri* where used, and may also be used at suggested points within the psalm 'in order to facilitate responsorial use'. Traditionally in the Church of England psalms have been said or sung either communally or antiphonally (leader and congregation, or the two sides of choir or congregation). In recent years, however, with the decline in the use of Anglican chant, the method has grown of the main text being said by a reader or sung by a cantor, with the congregation's part being reduced to joining in the refrain. This has perhaps been practised most commonly with the psalm at the eucharist, where this is used. It has the practical advantage that the congregation does not need to have the full text of the psalmody, and makes fewer musical demands on the congregation, but it has the disadvantage of depriving the congregation of full participation in the psalmody, which is meant to be part of the prayer of the people.

A different disadvantage arises in the use of metrical versions of the psalms, in which the constraints of metre inevitably entail a less accurate rendering of the words of the psalms, even where interpretative modifications are avoided. The obvious practical advantages of metrical psalms for congregational singing no doubt account for their popularity in the reformed churches, but the Anglican formularies have practically entirely refrained from adopting them, a permissive reference to the possibility of using a metrical version in the Note on Psalms in A Service of the Word (CW main book, p. 27) being the exception. Anglican preference has been definitely in favour of the use of prose texts, which can be sung to plainsong, Anglican chant, or a simple eight-note pattern of four half-verses, each with a reciting note and an inflexion on the final word(s). The practical difficulties of congregational singing of Anglican chant have been grossly exaggerated; all that is required is the provision of a pointed text for the congregation (as in the ASB of 1980), and the basic method could be taught in a single congregational practice. The singing of the whole text by the congregation certainly seems to cohere best with the Anglican tradition of 'common' prayer and worship, although the integrity of the text is also preserved in the use of responsorial psalms, although at the cost of severely limiting the congregation's participation. Some forms of metrical psalms, such as Isaac Watts' 'The heavens declare thy glory, Lord' (based on Ps. 19) or 'Jesus shall reign' (based on Ps. 72) are by no means to be despised, but are better recognized as Christian compositions inspired by the psalms than as actual psalm texts, and are more appropriately used as hymns.

As we conclude this account of the use of the psalms in the worship of the Church of England since the Reformation we note first of all their abiding centrality in Anglican tradtion. We notice too an extension in the use of psalmody, particularly at the Eucharist, and also in connection with some of the occasional services, in the more recent revisions. There has also been a growing degree of flexibility and the provision of different options, particularly in the CW services. In no sense can those responsible for the provision of orders of service at any period be accused of any attempt to reduce the use of psalmody in Anglican worship. Yet the reality of practice in many congregations gives ground for serious concern, in that many worshippers nowadays attend only the Eucharist or informal Family Services, and in many cases, despite the provisions of our formularies, experience little or no use of the psalms. They are in danger of being a part of the Scriptures which is for practical purposes being excluded from the canon of worship! This is a serious development in practice, unintended by our liturgical authorities, but with the potential of seriously weakening the character and content of our worship.

5. Conclusion

Why should the Church continue to use the Psalms in its worship? In his lecture 'Benedict and the Worship of the Church Today' Michael Perham offered four reasons for doing so.[18] The first is the Christological reason: the Psalms were the prayer book of Jesus during his earthly life, and, if we are to enter his mind, we too need the pray the Psalms as he did. This remains true, even if it cannot be demonstrated that Jesus used the whole of the Psalter.[19] The second is the realism of the Psalms. They express the whole range of human emotions, including in particular the elements of lament, bewilderment, and the audacity to protest against God. The third recognizes the Psalms as not only human address to God, but also as a part of the divine revelation, the Word of God to us. The fourth reason is the 'rhythm of psalmody that stills the body and quietens the soul'. To these reasons may be added others, in particular the practice of the universal church including the early Reformation period.

Against this the contemporary experience of much of the Church of England gives ground for considerable concern. Morning and Evening Prayer are no longer the normative services to which congregations are most accustomed. Many Anglican worshippers today are familiar only with eucharistic or family services. CW makes provision for an element of psalmody alongside the Scripture readings at every celebration of the Eucharist, and, in its directions for 'A Service of the Word', which includes family services, it specifies that a psalm or psalms, or occasionally a 'scriptural song', should normally be included (CW main book, p. 27, n. 6). It is very doubtful whether this ideal is widely practised. In the writer's limited personal experience the use of psalmody at the Sunday eucharist is the exception rather than the rule. As for what is often called 'all-age worship', it may be doubted how suitable the use of psalmody may be at all. Many regular Anglican churchgoers nowadays will probably encounter psalms only indirectly, in the form of hymns which happen to be metrical versions of psalms, and will be unlikely to distinguish them from other hymns. This indirect experience of psalmody will be quite haphazard, and worshippers will be unaware of psalmody as a distinct component of Christian worship.

---

[18] See note 6 on p23.
[19] See Paul Bradshaw, *Two ways of praying: Introducing liturgical spirituality* (SPCK, 1995) p. 75.

This disquiet is only increased when account is taken of occasional services. The use of a psalm at weddings is optional in CW, and in practice rare. At funerals a psalm *'should normally be used'* (CW *Pastoral Services*, p. 291, n. 2), and is still not uncommon, but a number of funeral services, even for church members, now contain no psalm. Most serious of all, in the writer's view, is the fact that services attended by many clergy, such as the Maundy Thursday 'Chrism Eucharist' with the renewal of ordination vows, are often celebrated without any psalmody at all. If psalms are regarded in practice as dispensable on such occasions as these, what hope is there for any regular use and experience of psalmody at Sunday services attended by the ordinary churchgoer?

The central importance of psalmody in the orders for *Daily Prayer* is the most encouraging feature in the present situation. At least in religious communities, and among the clergy who are under obligation to recite or join in the daily office, the Psalter will continue to be an important part of the daily diet of worship. The popularity of Choral Evensong in cathedrals and collegiate churches, particularly with the wider public, will ensure that many of the laity will not become completely unfamiliar with psalmody, even if they are not encouraged actually to join in singing the psalms! Many regular Anglican churchgoers, however, will remain outside these spheres, and for them there is a grave danger of the Psalter becoming an unknown territory. The loss to the spiritual development of individual churchmen, and to the quality of Anglican worship in general, would be incalculable. Those who worked to produce the CW services have tried valiantly to preserve and even enhance the use of psalmody in contemporary Anglican worship. It is up to ordinary clergy and churchpeople to make use of these provisions, if we are not to cut ourselves off from an element of Christian worship that has been, until recently, practically universal.

Appendix: For Further Reading

There is a vast literature on the Psalms, and there is space in this volume only to mention a handful of items that may be helpful to the general reader. Most of them contain further bibliographical references to enable the student to pursue the subject further.

John Day, *Psalms* (Old Testament Guides, Sheffield Academic Press, 1990)
This is a short introduction to the Psalms as a book within the Old Testament, and provides the general reader with a clear outline of modern scholarly approaches to this book.

John Eaton, *The Psalms: A historical and Spiritual Commentary with an Introduction and New Translation* (T & T Clark, 2003).
This commentary is specially recommended for a study of the psalms in the context of worship, both Jewish and Christian, and for its devotional content.

H. F. D. Sparks, 'Jerome as Biblical Scholar' in P. R. Ackroyd and C. F. Evans (edd), *The Cambridge History of the Bible, volume 1: From the Beginnings to Jerome* (Cambridge University Press, 1970) pp. 510-541. This is a useful outline of Jerome's important contribution to the transmission and interpretation of the Bible, and his three translations of the Psalter.

John A. Lamb, *The Psalms in Christian Worship* (Faith Press, 1962)
This is a classic historical survey, covering the Psalms in Hebrew Worship, in the New Testament, in the Early Church, the Eastern and Western Churches, the Lutheran, Reformed, and Anglican Churches, and ending with the author's own Church of Scotland.

G. G. Willis, *St. Augustine's Lectionary* (ACC 44, Alcuin/ SPCK, 1966)
This is a fascinating study of the gradual emergence of lectionaries, and of what can be gleaned from Augustine's own sermons about actual readings in his time.

Reginald Box, SSF, *Make Music to our God: How we sing the Psalms* (ACC 74, Alcuin/SPCK, 1996) This is a survey, both scholarly and practical, of methods of using the psalms in worship, with particular emphasis on methods of singing them, an aspect of the subject for which there has been little space in the present work.

Paul F. Bradshaw, *Daily Prayer in the Early Church* (ACC 63, Alcuin/SPCK, 1981) This is a ground-breaking study with copious references to primary sources, and a major critical contribution to what is often an elusive subject.

Robert Taft, SJ, *The Liturgy of the Hours in East and West* (Liturgical Press. Collegeville, 1986) This is a classic survey of the origins and later development of the Divine Office, which has always been the area of Christian worship in which the Psalms have pride of place.

Paul Bradshaw, *Two ways of praying: Introducing liturgical spirituality* (SPCK, 1995) This is a popular work spelling out the difference in ethos between the 'Cathedral' and 'Monastic' traditions of daily worship, and forms an excellent introduction to readers unfamiliar with this distinction.

The Alcuin Club
promoting liturgical scholarship and renewal

Eucharistic Origins
by Paul Bradshaw
*a challenging account of what can and cannot be known
about the origins of the Eucharist*
(SPCK 2004 - ISBN 0-281-05615-3 - £17.50)

Christian Prayer through the Centuries
by Joseph Jungmann
a new English translation of a liturgical classic
(SPCK 2007 - ISBN 0-281-05759-7 - £9.99)

The Companion to Common Worship (two volumes)
edited by Paul Bradshaw
*a detailed discussion of the origins and development
of each Common Worship rite
together with a comprehensive commentary on the text*
(Volume 1, SPCK 2001 - ISBN 0-281-05266-2 - £19.99)
(Volume 2, SPCK 2006 - ISBN 0-281-052778-8 - £19.99)

Celebrating the Eucharist
by Benjamin Gordon-Taylor & Simon Jones
*a popular and practical guide to the celebration
of the modern Eucharistic rite*
(SPCK 2005 - ISBN 0-281-05588-2 - £9.99)

The Use of Symbols in Worship
edited by Christopher Irvine
an account of the history of the liturgical use of
water, oil, light and incense
together with a practical guide
to using these symbols today
(SPCK 2007 - ISBN 0-281-05852-5- £9.99)

Celebrating Christ's Appearing
by Benjamin Gordon-Taylor & Simon Jones
celebrating the Christian year
from Advent to Candlemas
(SPCK 2008 - ISBN 0-281-05978-2 - £9.99)

To order any of these titles, or for details of how to join the Alcuin Club, email alcuinclub@gmail.com or telephone 01745 730585.
For all full list of Alcuin titles, go to www.alcuinclub.org.uk
Generous discounts available to members.

Alcuin/GROW Joint Liturgical Studies

48-56 pages, £5.95 in 2008. Nos 1-58 by Grove Books Ltd, Ridley Hall Road, Cambridge CB3 9HU

Nos. 4,9 and 16 are out of print. Nos 59 and following are published by Hymns Ancient and Modern (previously named SCM-CanterburyPress Ltd) – see outside back cover

Grove Liturgical Studies

These Studies of 32-40 pages ran in 1975-86, published or distributed by Grove Books Ltd. Price in 2008, £2.95

Grove Books Ltd, Ridley Hall Road, Cambridge CB3 9HU
Tel: 012223-464748 www.grovebooks.co.uk